MAYER SMITH

A Crown of Moonlit Thorns

Contents

One

The Forbidden Moon

The moon hung low in the night sky, its pale light casting long, eerie shadows across the dense forest. Elara stood at the edge of the clearing, her breath a mist that dissolved into the crisp, cool air. The scent of damp earth and pine wrapped around her, a familiar embrace in the stillness of the night. But tonight, the woods felt different. It wasn't the usual quiet she sought, the peace that soothed her restless mind. No, tonight there was an electricity in the air, a tension that hummed just beneath the surface.

The moon, full and unyielding, called to her. She could feel its pull in the pit of her stomach, the way it seemed to throb with the beat of her own heart. Something was coming. She could feel it deep in her bones.

Turning her gaze back to the path that led to the village, Elara's pulse quickened. She had not meant to come here tonight. The forest, where her ancestors once roamed, had always been a place of refuge. But the truth was—she had been avoiding it, avoiding the legends and the weight of the curse that hung over her bloodline. The curse that had followed her family for centuries. A curse that now felt so close, she could almost taste it.

"Elara…"

The whisper of her name was so soft, it might have been the wind. But she knew better.

She didn't turn immediately. The voice carried an unfamiliar weight—a darkness she hadn't expected to find in these woods. When she finally did, her heart skipped a beat. He was standing there, emerging from the shadows like a ghost, his tall frame silhouetted against the moonlight. Cael.

His eyes, like twin pools of midnight, fixed on her with an intensity that made her breath catch. She had seen him before, in the village, always just at the edge of her vision, always too far to reach, but never out of her thoughts. A mystery wrapped in shadow, Cael was the kind of man who made you wonder if the legends had any truth to them.

But that wasn't the reason her pulse surged in her veins. It wasn't just his striking presence or the way his dark hair fell messily across his brow, or how his jaw tensed as he watched her with those penetrating eyes. No, it was the knowledge that he knew something she didn't—a secret buried beneath the weight of her family's curse.

"Why are you here?" Her voice, though steady, betrayed her wariness. She could feel her skin tightening, a shiver running down her spine as his gaze never wavered.

"I could ask you the same thing," he replied, his tone low, almost teasing, though there was an undercurrent of something darker lurking beneath. "This place—it's not for people like you."

Elara frowned, her fingers tightening around the pendant she wore—a small silver crescent moon that her mother had given her, the only heirloom she had left. The weight of it, cold against her skin, comforted her, but there was an unease in her chest that refused to settle.

"And what kind of people would that be?" she asked, her voice clipped. The wind rustled the leaves around them, a soft, almost mournful sigh that seemed to echo her growing tension.

"The kind who don't understand what they're really up against."

He stepped forward, his boots making no sound against the forest floor, as though he were as much a part of the night as the trees themselves. His presence was unnerving—too calculated, too controlled. And yet, there was something magnetic about him, something that made Elara's heart flutter, even as her mind screamed for caution.

"Why do you follow me?" she asked, her voice no longer steady. She was angry, but the question came out more like a plea. She didn't want to be alone in this. Not tonight.

Cael's eyes softened for the briefest moment, before the darkness returned. "You're not alone. You never were." He said it so quietly that it almost sounded like a confession.

The words lingered between them, charged with an undeniable weight. Elara's heart beat faster, but it wasn't from fear alone. There was something else, something dangerous, pulling her in.

She could feel the moon above them, its cold light flooding the clearing, the silence between them filled only by the soft rustling of the trees. The world felt suspended, as though the air itself held its breath. Cael took another step, closer this time, until there was only a hair's breadth between them. She could see the faintest flicker of something in his eyes, something unreadable.

"Elara," he said her name again, this time it was almost a caress, soft but intense. He reached out, the tips of his fingers brushing against her wrist. A jolt of electricity ran up her arm, and she nearly flinched, but didn't pull away.

Her gaze flickered from his hand to his face, and for the first time, she saw the vulnerability there. A man who had been carved from shadows, yet beneath that dark exterior, something raw and desperate pulsed.

He looked at her as though he was searching for something in her—answers, perhaps. Or maybe he was asking her to save him, even though she was the one who didn't know how to save herself.

"What are you hiding from me, Cael?" Her voice was barely a whisper now, the air thick with the questions she had kept buried. "Why are you here?"

For a long moment, he didn't answer. His gaze dropped to her lips, and she felt the pull of his attention like a physical force. Her breath hitched, her chest tightening in response to the raw intensity between them. She knew she should back away, step out of the circle of his influence, but her feet were rooted to the ground.

"The curse," Cael said, his voice gravelly, like it was hard for him to speak the words. "It's coming for you, Elara. And there's nothing you can do to stop it."

The moonlight seemed to grow colder, the shadows around them deepening. Elara's heart thundered in her chest as the weight of his words settled over her like a storm. The curse. It was always there, just beyond the edges of her awareness, but hearing it spoken out loud made it real. More real than she wanted it to be.

"But…" She could barely find her voice. "I thought it was just a story. A myth."

Cael stepped back slightly, running a hand through his hair in frustration. "No, Elara. It's not. And you don't understand what you're up against. The curse is tied to you, to your bloodline.

And now, it's awake."

Her mind spun with the implications of his words. The pull of the moon was too much to ignore. The weight of her family's history pressed down on her chest.

"What do you want from me?" she whispered, her heart a jagged mix of fear and something else she couldn't place.

Cael's gaze softened, and for a moment, there was a tenderness in his eyes that took her by surprise. "I don't want anything from you, Elara. I'm trying to protect you."

"From what?" Her voice cracked, the question too large for her to handle.

He didn't answer immediately. Instead, he stepped back, his eyes scanning the darkness around them. Something shifted in the trees. The wind stilled, and for a long, tense moment, Elara thought she saw a figure moving in the distance.

A presence. Closing in.

Cael turned back to her, his expression hardening. "We don't have time. They're coming for you."

The forest suddenly seemed too quiet, as though it held its breath, waiting for something terrible to happen. And Elara, standing there in the moonlight, knew—without a doubt—that nothing in her life would ever be the same again.

Two

Whispers of the Past

The air felt different this morning. It was thick with anticipation, hanging heavy in the spaces between breaths. Elara awoke to the soft murmur of the wind against the windowpane, carrying with it the scent of rain and earth. The sky outside was still gray, the clouds low and pregnant with the promise of a storm. It felt as though the world was holding its breath, waiting for something to break the stillness.

She lay in her bed for a moment longer, eyes fixed on the ceiling as the weight of Cael's words from the night before pulsed through her mind. The curse was real. It was tied to her bloodline, to the very essence of who she was. How had she not known? How had her family allowed her to live in blissful ignorance? The questions spiraled, each one more maddening than the last. But the hardest question to answer was the one that lingered beneath the surface: Why had Cael come into her life now?

She could still feel the ghost of his touch on her wrist, the way his fingers had brushed against her skin, like a spark setting fire to everything she had thought she knew. A chill ran down her spine. She hadn't imagined the intensity in his eyes, the desperation that had flashed there when he spoke of the curse. The way he'd seemed so certain that she was already entangled in its web.

But even as fear gripped her, something else had stirred within her—a pull, an undeniable connection to him. Elara had never believed in fate, never thought much of destiny, but there was something about Cael that defied logic. He was a mystery wrapped in darkness, and she found herself inexplicably drawn to him.

Rolling out of bed, Elara padded quietly across the cold wooden floor of her room. Her mother's old oak desk stood against the far wall, the surface cluttered with papers, old maps, and books on the family's lineage. Elara's fingers brushed over the spines of the worn leather-bound volumes, the faint scent of old parchment filling the air. It was here, in this room, that she had learned the stories of her ancestors—of the strange and twisted history that her family had kept hidden for so long.

She had never truly believed the stories. They had always felt like folklore, something meant to scare children, not the truth. But now, with the weight of Cael's revelation pressing down on her, she wasn't so sure anymore.

Her fingers hovered over a thick tome that lay open on the desk. It was an ancient record, a history of the bloodline that she had inherited, passed down through generations. She had read parts of it before, but it had always seemed like distant, half-remembered tales from another time. Now, though, it felt too real. As if the very words on the page were alive, watching her, waiting for her to uncover their meaning.

Elara's hand shook as she turned the fragile pages, each one crinkling under her touch. She stopped at a page with an intricate illustration of the moon, its silver light casting long, dark shadows. Beneath the drawing was a passage written in flowing script:

"The blood of the moon is a gift and a curse. Those born under its light shall forever be bound to its pull, their fate intertwined with the ebb and flow of the tide. The curse will awaken in the dark of night, and the moon shall bear witness to the fall of the one who carries its mark."

Elara's breath caught in her throat. The words seemed to vibrate in the air around her, heavy with meaning. Her eyes flicked to the moon pendant around her neck, the one her mother had given her when she was just a child. It had always been a symbol of her family's legacy, a reminder of the strength they carried. But now, it felt like a tether to something darker, something she wasn't sure she was ready to face.

A sudden knock on her door broke the silence, and Elara quickly closed the book, hiding it beneath a stack of papers. She forced a smile as she turned to face the intruder.

Her younger brother, Alistair, stood in the doorway, his eyes wide with concern. "You're up early," he said, his voice thick with sleep. His hair was rumpled, and he still wore the faded clothes from the night before. He had always been the more carefree of the two, his spirit lighter than hers, but there was something different in the way he looked at her now—an unease that she couldn't quite place.

"I couldn't sleep," Elara admitted, crossing the room to join him. She placed a hand on his shoulder, trying to offer comfort, though she wasn't sure she could give it. "I had a lot on my mind."

He studied her for a moment, his brow furrowing. "Are you still thinking about the dream?"

Elara froze. Her pulse quickened at the mention of the dream. The one that had haunted her for days now. The one that had started after her encounter with Cael. In the dream, she was standing in a forest, the same forest where she had met him, but it was darker, twisted in a way that made it feel like the trees themselves were watching her. She could feel eyes on her, the weight of the moon's gaze pressing down on her, suffocating her. And then, as if in answer to her fear, Cael would appear—his eyes full of secrets, full of warnings. Always just out of reach.

"I don't know," Elara whispered. "I keep seeing the same things. The forest. The moon. And..." She hesitated, her breath catching in her throat. "And him."

Alistair didn't say anything at first. His eyes flicked to the window, where the pale light of the morning filtered through the curtains. He seemed lost in thought for a moment, before turning back to her with a mixture of confusion and worry.

"Elara…" He began slowly, as if he were choosing his words carefully. "You've been distant lately. I can feel it. Is there something you're not telling me?"

She opened her mouth to respond but stopped herself. What could she say? That she was beginning to question everything she had ever known about herself? That the curse her family had kept hidden was more than just a myth? That the man she couldn't stop thinking about—Cael—was somehow tied to it all?

Instead, she gave him a tight smile. "I'm fine. I'm just… thinking about some things."

He didn't seem convinced, but he didn't press further. Instead, he nodded and stepped back. "Well, don't think too hard. You've got a busy day ahead of you."

Elara watched him leave, her gaze lingering on the door long after it had closed. Her heart felt heavy, burdened with the weight of the secrets she was beginning to uncover. She couldn't escape the sense that something was coming, something dark and inevitable, and she wasn't sure if she was strong enough to face it.

The rest of the day passed in a blur. Elara went through the motions—meeting with the village elders, helping her mother in the garden, even exchanging pleasantries with the few friends she had left. But her mind was elsewhere. It always was now, drifting back to Cael, to the curse, to the strange, unshakable feeling that the world was closing in around her.

When evening fell and the moon rose once more, Elara couldn't shake the feeling that the night was waiting for her. Waiting to reveal something. She had to know more. She had to find out what Cael wasn't telling her.

But as she moved to leave the house, she paused by the window, her hand resting on the cool glass. Outside, the night was thick with mist, the trees cloaked in shadow. And in the distance, just beyond the treeline, she thought she saw a figure standing in the darkness, watching her.

Her heart skipped a beat.

It was Cael.

Three

The Moon's Embrace

The night hung thick with fog, as though the moon itself had shrouded the world in a veil of mystery. Elara stood at the window, watching the slow crawl of shadows across the land, her fingers tracing the outline of the moon pendant that hung from her neck. The silver crescent felt colder tonight, its presence almost a weight rather than a comfort. The air was heavy with a promise, a dark promise, one that made her skin prickle with unease.

She had tried to ignore the moon's pull, but it was becoming impossible to deny. The dreams had escalated, the forest more oppressive, the shadows more alive. And it wasn't just the dreams. It was the way the forest seemed to whisper to her, the way the wind tugged at her hair, and the trees seemed to lean closer as if urging her to step deeper into their embrace.

Her thoughts returned to Cael. He had been distant since their meeting, and yet, she couldn't shake the feeling that he was always just beyond her reach, watching her, waiting. There had been moments, too many moments, where she caught him staring at her, his gaze intense, as though he were searching for something in her eyes. But what? She wasn't sure.

"Are you going to stand there all night?"

The voice broke through her reverie, causing Elara to jump. She turned to find her brother Alistair standing in the doorway, his expression one of concern. He had always been able to tell when something was wrong, even if she didn't say a word.

"What is it?" she asked, forcing a smile as she turned away from the window. The last thing she wanted was for him to see the turmoil she was feeling, the confusion that had taken root deep within her chest.

"You've been restless for days," he said, his tone soft but insistent. "I can tell. You're not sleeping. You're not yourself."

Elara sighed, her shoulders heavy as if the weight of her thoughts was physically bearing down on her. "It's nothing," she said quickly, brushing past him. "Just… everything has been overwhelming lately."

Alistair's eyes narrowed, but he didn't push. Instead, he walked over to her, his steps light but deliberate. "If it's about him—Cael—I don't trust him, Elara."

Her heart skipped a beat. Of course, he was going to mention Cael. He had always been protective of her, and the sudden appearance of the enigmatic stranger in her life hadn't gone unnoticed by him. But her brother's suspicion only added to the confusion she felt. She didn't know who to trust anymore, least of all herself.

"It's not just him," she said, her voice shaking slightly. "It's everything. The dreams... the curse. It's all real, Alistair. I've seen it."

His brows furrowed in confusion. "What are you talking about?"

"The curse," she repeated, her voice barely a whisper. "It's in our blood. It's always been there."

Alistair stepped closer, his expression softening with concern. "You're scaring me. The curse—those are just stories, Elara. Myths. You don't believe them, do you?"

Elara hesitated, her gaze shifting to the window once more. The moon hung high in the sky, its pale light casting long shadows that seemed to stretch across the land. It was as though it was waiting, watching, a silent witness to everything that was about to unfold.

"I don't know what to believe anymore," she said quietly, her voice tinged with fear. "But I think we're running out of time."

Alistair didn't reply, and for a long moment, the only sound in the room was the faint rustling of the wind outside. Elara could feel the weight of her brother's stare, but she couldn't meet his eyes. The truth was, she didn't want to believe in the curse either. She didn't want to believe that her bloodline had been marked by something so dark and inevitable. But the more she learned, the more it felt as though there was no escape. The more she tried to push it away, the stronger the pull became.

"I'll be fine," she said finally, more to herself than to Alistair. "I just need some time to think."

Without waiting for a response, she left the room, moving down the narrow hallway of their family's cottage. The house was small, cozy, but tonight it felt too confining, as though the walls themselves were closing in. She had to get out. She needed to breathe.

Stepping outside, the chill of the night air hit her like a slap to the face, and she pulled her cloak tighter around her shoulders. The village was quiet, the streets nearly deserted as most people were already inside, their homes warm with the glow of lanterns. The only sound was the soft rustling of leaves and the distant howl of a lone wolf. The fog from earlier had thickened, curling around her feet like tendrils, obscuring the path ahead.

She started walking, drawn to the forest again, as though the trees themselves were calling her. It wasn't a conscious decision, but before she knew it, she found herself standing at the edge of the woods, looking into the darkness that lay beyond. The shadows seemed to shift and writhe, as though they were alive, watching her.

And then, out of the corner of her eye, she saw him. Cael.

He was standing just beyond the treeline, his form barely visible in the fog, but the intensity of his gaze cut through the mist like a blade. It was as if he had been waiting for her, waiting for the moment when she would finally come to him.

"Elara."

His voice was low, almost a whisper, but it sent a shiver through her body. She hadn't realized how badly she had been hoping to see him, how much she had been longing for some answer, for some explanation.

"What are you doing here?" she asked, her voice trembling despite her best efforts to sound confident.

Cael stepped forward, his movement fluid and effortless, as though the fog parted for him. "I could ask you the same thing," he replied, his tone unreadable. His eyes locked onto hers, and for a moment, Elara forgot how to breathe. The pull between them was undeniable, magnetic, and it left her feeling both terrified and exhilarated.

"I came to find you," she said before she could stop herself. It wasn't just a statement; it was a confession, a truth she hadn't even realized she had been holding inside.

Cael's lips curved into a faint smile, but it didn't reach his eyes. "I'm not surprised," he murmured, his voice darker now, tinged with something dangerous. "You can't fight it, Elara. You can't fight the pull of the moon. It's part of who you are."

She swallowed, her heart pounding in her chest. "I don't understand. What does all of this mean? Why me?"

Cael's gaze flicked to the sky, his face briefly illuminated by the moonlight that cut through the fog. "You're the key," he said, his voice low, filled with an intensity that left her breathless. "The moon's blood flows through your veins. You're not like the others. And it's time you learned the truth."

Elara felt her pulse quicken, her head spinning with the implications of his words. The truth? What truth? She opened her mouth to ask more, but before she could speak, Cael stepped closer, his presence overwhelming, enveloping her in a way that left her dizzy.

"You don't have much time," he whispered, his lips brushing against her ear, sending a shock of warmth through her. "The curse is awakening, and when it does, it will claim you."

She wanted to pull away, to ask more, to demand answers, but instead, she found herself stepping closer to him. The pull between them was irresistible, and she couldn't fight it any longer.

But just as their lips were inches apart, a rustling sound echoed through the trees, breaking the spell. Elara froze, her heart racing as she looked over her shoulder. The moment had passed, and with it, the strange, magnetic connection she had shared with Cael.

He stepped back, his face unreadable once again, and the fog swallowed him whole.

"Elara," his voice called out from the mist, low and final. "Remember, you're not alone. But time is running out."

Four

Betrayal in the Shadows

The moon was hidden behind a blanket of thick clouds, leaving the night in complete darkness, save for the flickering lights of the village lanterns. Elara's breath came in shallow, uneven bursts as she made her way down the narrow alley that wound through the outskirts of the village. The streets, usually filled with the sounds of lively chatter, were eerily quiet. The usual hum of the town had been replaced by an unsettling silence, broken only by the distant rustle of the wind and the occasional creak of a wooden sign swaying in the breeze.

She had hoped the night would be different. She had hoped that after her meeting with Cael, she would have found some clarity, some sense of peace. But all she felt was the weight of his words pressing down on her chest, and the nagging feeling that something was wrong. That she was being watched.

The woods were always close, always beckoning, but tonight, she had an errand to run. Her mother had sent her to deliver a package to one of the village elders—an old woman named Mirella, who had always been a bit too mysterious for Elara's liking. Mirella had been the one to first tell Elara's mother about the curse, years ago, and Elara had always found her warnings unsettling.

But tonight, the village felt different. It wasn't just the absence of life on the streets. It was the way the air tasted—stale, almost metallic—and the way the trees loomed on the edge of the village, their silhouettes dark and formless against the sky. It was as though the very earth beneath her feet had become unmoored, shifting and uncertain.

As she passed a narrow passage between two stone buildings, Elara froze, her heart racing in her chest. She wasn't alone.

A shadow moved in the corner of her eye, a dark figure flitting between the buildings. Her first instinct was to run, to turn and escape into the safety of her home, but something stopped her. She wasn't sure why. It could have been the way the figure had moved, so gracefully, like a predator stalking its prey—or perhaps it was the feeling that she knew the person, or rather, who the person was.

"Elara."

The voice was low and familiar, sending a shiver through her spine. It was him—Cael.

She turned slowly, her breath catching in her throat as she faced him, his silhouette emerging from the shadows like a ghost. His dark eyes gleamed in the dim light, his face a mask of calm that barely concealed the tension radiating off him. His presence seemed to fill the narrow alley, pressing in on her from all sides.

"What are you doing here?" she demanded, her voice edged with a mixture of irritation and something else she couldn't name.

Cael didn't answer immediately. He simply stepped closer, his movement fluid and silent. She could smell the faint scent of pine and carth on him, the same scent that had clung to his clothes the night they first met. It was strangely comforting and unnerving at the same time.

"I came to warn you," he said finally, his voice low, almost hoarse. "You're not safe here, Elara. You never were."

His words sent a jolt of unease through her, and she instinctively took a step back. She felt like a cornered animal, every sense on high alert as the shadows seemed to press in closer.

"What do you mean?" she whispered, her throat dry. "Why now? What's going on?"

Cael's gaze flickered to the darkened windows of the nearby homes, as though he were checking for anyone who might be watching. His eyes hardened, his jaw clenching in a way that made Elara's heart pound faster.

"You're being followed," he said, his voice barely above a whisper. "There are eyes everywhere."

The words hit her like a punch to the gut. She glanced over her shoulder, her pulse quickening. She hadn't seen anyone, but the feeling of being watched was overwhelming. The hairs on the back of her neck stood on end as the weight of Cael's words sank in.

"I don't understand," she said, her voice trembling. "Why would anyone be watching me?"

Cael's expression softened for a brief moment, but there was something dark in his eyes. Something that made Elara feel as though she were standing on the edge of a precipice, staring into an abyss.

"You're not just anyone," he said quietly. "You're the heir to the curse, Elara. And those who want its power will stop at nothing to claim it."

Her breath caught in her throat. "What are you talking about? Who would want to claim it?"

He looked away for a moment, his eyes narrowing as if searching for the right words. When he spoke again, his voice was laced with an emotion she couldn't quite place. "The bloodline you carry… it's more than just a curse. It's a key. A key to power, Elara. And some people are willing to do anything to get their hands on it."

Her heart was hammering in her chest now, a cold sweat breaking out across her skin. The weight of his words pressed down on her, suffocating her. A key to power?

Before she could respond, a voice echoed from the darkness ahead—sharp, familiar, and full of menace.

"Elara."

Her body stiffened at the sound of her name. She spun around, her heart racing, and saw him standing there—Alistair. Her brother, his face pale in the dim light, his expression a mixture of fear and confusion.

"What are you doing here?" Elara's voice came out in a strangled gasp. The last thing she had expected was for him to show up at a time like this.

"I—I've been looking for you," Alistair said, his gaze flickering between her and Cael. "Something's wrong, Elara. Something's happening to the village."

Cael didn't move, didn't speak. He simply stood there, his gaze fixed on Alistair, a tension building in the air between them. The weight of the moment pressed down on Elara, and for the first time, she truly felt the depth of the divide between her two worlds. Her brother, whom she trusted above all else, and Cael, the enigmatic stranger who seemed to know more than he was letting on.

"Elara…" Alistair took a step closer, his voice low. "We need to go home. I don't feel safe here. The others—they're acting strange. There's something wrong with the villagers. They've been… watching."

Elara's heart dropped into her stomach. She looked back at Cael, her eyes searching his, looking for any sign of reassurance, but his expression remained unreadable.

"Go with him," Cael said, his voice low and urgent. "It's not safe for you to be out here alone."

She didn't know why, but for the briefest moment, she wanted to stay. Wanted to hear more from him. The way he spoke, the urgency in his eyes, it stirred something deep inside her—a need to know the truth, no matter how terrifying it might be.

But as she glanced back at Alistair, the look of concern in his eyes cut through her hesitation. Her brother needed her. She couldn't abandon him.

"Elara…" Alistair's voice was softer now, his hand reaching out to her. "Please."

With a final, lingering glance at Cael, Elara nodded, turning away from him. "Come on, Alistair," she said, her voice firm despite the unease that twisted in her gut. "We'll go back home."

But as they turned to leave, Elara couldn't shake the feeling that something was terribly wrong. That the darkness, the danger, was not just outside the village— but inside it. And the deeper she looked, the more she realized the truth: the very people she had trusted were hiding secrets. Secrets that could cost them everything.

And somewhere, in the shadows, those who wanted the curse's power were waiting. Watching.

Waiting for the right moment to strike.

Five

A Forbidden Alliance

The rain had started to fall heavily by the time Elara and Alistair reached the edge of the village. The sound of the downpour was deafening, a relentless hammering against the cobblestones, as though the heavens themselves were angry. Elara pulled her cloak tighter around her shoulders, trying in vain to shield herself from the cold, biting rain. But it didn't matter. The chill in her bones had little to do with the weather.

Her mind was still racing, the image of Cael lingering in the back of her thoughts, his cryptic warnings echoing through her head. The curse is awakening, he had said, his voice so urgent, so sure. You're not safe here. Not anymore. The weight of his words pressed down on her chest, squeezing the breath from her lungs. What had he meant by that? And why had he been watching her so closely? His touch, the pull she had felt when they were close—she couldn't deny that it had shaken her. Something deeper was stirring, something far beyond her understanding. But the feeling of being torn between fear and something far more dangerous, more consuming, gnawed at her constantly.

"Elara."

She turned toward Alistair's voice, the familiar sound of it anchoring her in the midst of the storm. He was standing a few paces behind her, looking at her with a mixture of concern and frustration. His brow was furrowed, and his dark hair clung to his forehead, plastered there by the rain.

"What is it?" she asked, her voice sharp despite herself.

"Talk to me," Alistair said, his voice softer now. He was close enough to reach out and touch her, but his hesitation was clear. "I don't understand what's going on with you. Since you came back from the forest, you've been different. You're not yourself."

She opened her mouth to respond, but the words caught in her throat. She couldn't tell him everything. She couldn't tell him about Cael, about the curse, about the feeling that something was watching them. It was too dangerous. He wouldn't understand. No one would.

"I'm fine," Elara lied, forcing a smile that didn't quite reach her eyes. "I'm just tired. That's all."

Alistair didn't seem convinced, but he didn't press further.

Instead, he nodded and turned toward the small cottage that was their home. "We should get inside. It's not safe out here in this storm."

Elara followed him without a word, her thoughts consumed by the encounter with Cael. The storm outside was nothing compared to the storm raging inside her. She could feel it—the magnetic pull that Cael had on her, the way he made her forget everything else. It scared her, but it exhilarated her too. The attraction, the tension between them—it was undeniable. But was it real, or was it something darker? Was he drawing her in for a reason she didn't yet understand?

As they neared the door, a figure stepped out from the shadows of the alleyway, blocking their path. Elara froze, her heart leaping into her throat. Her first instinct was to reach for the knife she kept hidden beneath her cloak, but she quickly realized who it was. Cael.

His dark, drenched form was silhouetted by the dim light spilling from the cottage windows. His hair was plastered to his face, his clothes soaked through, but there was no mistaking the intensity in his eyes. They gleamed, sharp and focused, as he looked at her with an intensity that made her breath catch.

"Elara," he said, his voice low and urgent, cutting through the storm's roar. "We need to talk."

Alistair stiffened, his hand instinctively moving to the hilt of his own knife. He wasn't used to seeing strangers in their village, especially not ones like Cael. "Who are you?" he demanded, his voice firm. "What do you want with my sister?"

Elara stepped forward, her hand touching Alistair's arm, urging him to relax. "He's not a threat," she said quickly, though she wasn't sure she entirely believed that herself.

Cael's gaze flicked between them, and for a brief moment, his lips curled into a slight, almost imperceptible smile. But the smile didn't reach his eyes. His focus remained on Elara.

"I'm not here to cause trouble," he said, his voice quieter now, tinged with an underlying urgency. "But you're in danger, Elara. And I need your help."

Elara glanced at Alistair, her mind racing. This was exactly what she had been afraid of—being dragged into something she didn't fully understand, something that she wasn't sure she was ready for. She could see the doubt in her brother's eyes, the way his hand clenched around the knife's hilt as he studied Cael.

"Elara," Cael repeated, his voice softer now, almost coaxing. "I'm not asking you to trust me—not yet. But if you don't come with me, if you don't take this seriously, it's not just your life at risk."

She felt a cold shiver run down her spine. The air between them seemed to hum with an electric tension, a pull that she couldn't explain. Her heart beat faster, her chest tightening. She didn't know what to do. She didn't know if she could trust him, if she should trust him. But she also knew that something was wrong, something beyond her ability to understand. And for reasons she couldn't explain, she felt like she had no choice but to follow him.

"Elara, don't," Alistair's voice broke through her thoughts, his warning sharp. "I don't trust him. You can't just go off with him. We don't know who he really is."

But the connection between her and Cael, the invisible thread that had pulled her to him from the moment they had met, was too strong to ignore. She took a deep breath and looked at her brother, her expression softening despite the fear gnawing at her.

"I'll be fine," she said, her voice quiet but resolute. "You don't need to worry about me."

Before Alistair could protest, she turned to Cael, her heart pounding in her chest. "What do you need from me?" she asked, her voice barely above a whisper.

Cael's gaze softened, the hardness in his eyes momentarily replaced with something more vulnerable. For a brief, fleeting moment, Elara saw the man beneath the shadow—the one who had been hurt, who had been searching for answers just as much as she had.

"There's no time to explain everything right now," he said. "But I need you to trust me. There are people in this village—people who want to use the curse. People who will stop at nothing to control it."

"Who?" Elara demanded, her voice tightening. "Who are they?"

He shook his head, a shadow crossing his face. "I can't tell you yet. But they're close. Closer than you think."

Elara's pulse quickened as she glanced back at Alistair. She could see the concern in his eyes, the fear. But she also knew that this was her path to walk. No matter how dangerous it was, she couldn't turn back now. She had to know the truth.

With a final, lingering glance at her brother, Elara turned to Cael. "Take me where we need to go."

Cael didn't speak, but his eyes softened, something passing between them. Without another word, he turned, moving swiftly through the rain-soaked streets. Elara followed, her steps echoing in the night. The storm raged on around them, but for the first time, Elara felt as though she were finally stepping into the heart of the mystery that had haunted her. The tension between her and Cael simmered, a slow burn that neither of them seemed willing—or able—to ignore. The deeper they went, the closer they came to whatever dark truth lay hidden just out of sight.

But Elara knew one thing for certain: once she crossed this threshold, there would be no turning back.

Six

The Price of Power

The sky was a deep, bruised purple as Elara walked beside Cael through the narrow, winding path that led deeper into the forest. The rain had stopped, but the damp earth beneath her feet still squelched with every step, and the air was thick with the scent of wet foliage and wood. The dense trees loomed overhead like ancient guardians, their twisted branches reaching out, creating a canopy so thick it seemed to swallow the light of the fading day.

With every step she took, the oppressive weight of the forest seemed to close in around her, as if the very earth was watching, listening. She couldn't shake the feeling that they were not alone, that eyes were on them, waiting, lurking just out of sight. But when she glanced around, all she saw were the shadows of trees and the soft rustling of leaves in the faint breeze.

Beside her, Cael moved like a shadow himself, his every step calculated and silent, as though he knew this forest intimately, as though he belonged to it in a way Elara never could. His presence, so close and yet so distant, sent a shiver down her spine. His dark hair was still damp from the rain, falling messily over his forehead, but there was no mistaking the intensity in his eyes. He was always watching, always aware. There was something about him that made her feel as though he saw straight through her, as though he could read every thought, every secret she had hidden deep within.

"Elara," his voice broke through her thoughts, low and soft, yet carrying a weight that made her heart skip a beat. "The truth you're seeking—it comes at a price."

She turned her head to look at him, her breath catching at the intensity of his gaze. "What do you mean?" Her voice trembled slightly despite her best efforts to sound composed.

Cael slowed his pace for a moment, his gaze flickering to the path ahead as if weighing his words. He wasn't used to revealing anything about himself—not to her, at least. And yet, something in his expression now made her wonder if, just maybe, he was starting to let her in. A small, fleeting vulnerability, but it was there—if only for a second.

"The curse that's tied to your bloodline," he said, his voice low, almost a whisper. "It's not just some old legend. It's real. But it's more than just a burden. It's a key. A key to power beyond your understanding, Elara. Power that people will kill for."

She could feel the weight of his words settling on her chest, pushing the air from her lungs. She had always known there was something dark and ancient tied to her family's name, but to hear Cael speak of it so plainly—so ominously—left her feeling unmoored. The curse, she had thought, was just a tale told by the elders to keep the younger ones in line, something to scare children into obedience. But now, with every word he spoke, the edges of the story she had known began to fray, revealing a much darker truth.

"A key to power?" Her voice faltered, a ripple of fear threading through her. "What kind of power? And who—who would want it?"

Cael didn't answer immediately. Instead, he turned his gaze to the darkening sky above, his jaw tightening as if wrestling with something—an emotion he wasn't willing to share, or perhaps something he didn't fully understand himself.

"The kind of power that bends kingdoms to its will," he said, his voice edged with bitterness. "The kind of power that can control life and death itself. It's an ancient magic, one that has been buried for centuries, locked away in bloodlines like yours. You're a vessel, Elara. A living conduit for that power. And there are those who will stop at nothing to claim it."

The words sent a chill through her, as if she had just stepped into a shadow darker than the forest itself. She felt her heart rate quicken, but she refused to let the fear show on her face. She couldn't afford to show weakness—not now, when she was on the precipice of discovering something that might change everything.

"So what is it you're asking me to do?" Her voice was steady, but the question hung heavy in the air between them. Her chest tightened with the realization that this wasn't just about breaking a curse anymore. It was about survival.

Cael didn't immediately answer. Instead, he stepped closer, his dark eyes meeting hers with a sharp intensity. The sudden proximity sent an unexpected shiver through her, the heat from his body enveloping her like a wave, pulling her deeper into the gravity of his presence. Her pulse fluttered in her neck, and despite herself, she felt her breath catch.

"I need your trust," he said softly, his voice barely above a whisper, but there was something in his tone that made her heart race. "I need you to come with me. We need to find the source—the heart of the curse—before they do. If they get to it first, it will be too late. All of us will be lost."

Elara swallowed hard, her throat dry. She could feel the weight of the decision pressing down on her, like a hand closing around her chest. Her head was spinning with all that she had learned, with the uncertainty of Cael's intentions, and the strange, undeniable pull she felt toward him.

"I don't know if I can trust you," she whispered, the words slipping from her lips before she could stop them. She hated herself for saying it, but the truth of it stung, burning in her chest.

Cael's expression flickered for just a moment—surprise, maybe, or perhaps a brief flicker of hurt—but it was gone before Elara could make sense of it. He didn't speak at first, his gaze still locked on hers, as though searching for something.

"You don't have to trust me," he finally said, his voice steady now. "You just need to trust the truth. The curse is alive, Elara. And it's coming for you."

The finality of his words hung between them, like a silent declaration. She had felt the truth of it in her bones the moment she had stepped into the forest with him, in the way her heart had started to race whenever he was near, in the way his presence seemed to electrify the very air around them.

But now, as he spoke, something else stirred deep within her—a burning curiosity, a desire to understand, to unravel the mystery that had tied her to this strange man, to the power that lay dormant in her veins. She didn't know why, but she had this feeling that her fate, whatever it was, had always been tied to him. That they were two pieces of some puzzle, one that neither of them had been able to solve until now.

"What do we need to do?" she asked, her voice barely above a whisper.

Cael's lips curled into a faint, knowing smile. There was a brief flash of something unreadable in his eyes—satisfaction, perhaps, or something darker—and it made her heart skip a beat.

"There's a ritual," he said. "A way to access the full power of the curse. But it's dangerous. If we're not careful, it could destroy everything."

The air around them seemed to hum with the promise of something dangerous, something that would change everything. Elara's chest tightened, her mind racing. She wasn't ready for this. She wasn't ready to walk into the heart of the darkness, to risk everything for the truth. But then she remembered the way Cael had looked at her—the way his presence had filled the spaces between them, and she knew.

She had no choice.

"We'll do it," she said, her voice steady, though her heart was anything but. "We'll stop them."

Cael's gaze softened, and for the briefest moment, Elara saw something in him—a flicker of something human, something beyond the shadows and the secrets. It was gone before she could reach for it, but the fleeting glimpse left her unsettled. She wasn't sure whether it was hope or fear that twisted in her chest.

He nodded slowly, his face serious once more. "Then we have no time to waste. The heart of the curse is closer than you think."

Seven

The Silent Hunter

The moon was high in the sky, a silver disc hanging in the inky blackness above the dense forest canopy. Elara could feel the weight of its gaze, cold and unyielding, as though the heavens themselves were watching her every move. The air was heavy with moisture, thick with the scent of damp earth and decaying leaves. The path before her was dark, the shadows swallowing the edges of the trail, leaving nothing but the soft crunch of twigs beneath her boots.

She had been walking for what felt like hours, though the forest had a way of distorting time, making it feel both endless and suffocating. Her cloak clung to her wet skin, the cold of the night seeping through, but it wasn't the chill that had her on edge. It was the silence—the unnerving stillness that hung like a shroud over everything. Even the wind had gone still, as though the world had held its breath, waiting for something. Watching.

Beside her, Cael moved with practiced ease, his dark form blending into the shadows, his presence as quiet and unsettling as the forest itself. He didn't speak much these days, and when he did, his words were laced with warning, with an urgency that felt foreign to her. Something had shifted in him since their last conversation, something more than just the weight of their mission. He was distant—colder than before—but there was still that pull, that magnetic force that seemed to draw her in every time he glanced at her, every time their hands brushed. It left her confused, torn between fear and a desire she didn't fully understand.

"Do you feel that?" Elara asked, her voice a whisper, barely audible over the sound of her own breathing. The words seemed to hang in the air between them, swallowed by the vast expanse of trees.

Cael didn't answer right away. His eyes were scanning the shadows ahead, his face set in a hard, unreadable expression. He had been silent for most of the journey, as if lost in thought, or perhaps listening to something she couldn't hear. Finally, he turned to her, his lips curling into a faint, knowing smile.

"You're not imagining things," he said quietly, his voice low, his tone serious. "We're not alone."

Elara's heart skipped a beat, and she instinctively tightened her grip on the dagger hidden beneath her cloak. "Who's out there?" she asked, her voice betraying a hint of panic. "Are they following us?"

Cael's gaze flickered toward the trees, his eyes narrowing as if searching for something. "I don't know," he said, his voice tinged with caution. "But whoever it is, they're good. Too good. We've been walking into their trap for some time."

Elara swallowed hard, her throat dry. The air suddenly felt colder, as though the temperature had dropped several degrees in an instant. The hairs on the back of her neck stood on end, and the forest, which had once seemed like a haven, now felt like a prison, the trees closing in on them, whispering secrets she couldn't understand.

"Do you think we can make it out of here?" she asked, her voice barely a whisper, her heart pounding in her chest.

Cael didn't answer immediately, but when he did, his words were laced with an unsettling calm. "We'll have to. But there's no telling what's waiting for us on the other side."

They continued walking, the tension between them thickening with every step. The quiet of the forest was oppressive, the silence hanging heavy like a blanket over everything. And then, just as Elara thought she might go mad from the stillness, a sound—faint, but unmistakable—reached her ears. A soft, almost imperceptible rustle in the underbrush. A twig snapping, just out of reach. It was subtle, but it was enough to make her stop in her tracks.

"Did you hear that?" she whispered, her heart skipping a beat.

Cael nodded slightly, his eyes narrowing as he scanned the

darkness ahead of them. "They're close."

Before Elara could react, a flash of movement appeared in the corner of her vision. She whipped her head around, her heart leaping into her throat as she tried to make sense of what she was seeing. It was just a shadow, a fleeting figure darting between the trees, too fast for her to track.

She barely had time to react when Cael's hand shot out, grabbing her arm and pulling her toward him. His grip was firm, almost possessive, and for the briefest moment, she felt a strange flutter in her chest—something like a warning, a recognition of how close they had become over the course of their journey. But there was no time to focus on that now.

"Stay close," Cael murmured, his voice low and commanding, though there was a hint of something else beneath his words. An undercurrent of urgency. "We can't afford to be separated."

Elara nodded, her breath shallow as she allowed herself to be guided forward, moving swiftly but silently through the forest. Her senses were heightened, every crack of a twig, every whisper of movement, sending her heart into a frenzy. Whoever was following them wasn't making it easy. The hunter was no amateur; they moved with purpose, their steps carefully calculated, their presence concealed behind the thick veil of the trees.

The night seemed to stretch on forever, the forest dark and suffocating, but finally, they reached a clearing. The sudden openness was disorienting, the vastness of the sky above them almost dizzying after the claustrophobic confines of the trees. Elara felt her pulse quicken. This was it. This was where the hunter would make their move.

Cael stopped abruptly, pulling her to a halt beside him. His eyes scanned the clearing, his body tense, every muscle coiled like a predator waiting to strike. Elara could feel the shift in the air, the electric tension building with every passing second. Something was coming. She could feel it deep in her bones.

And then, as if on cue, the figure emerged from the shadows.

It was a man, tall and lean, his movements fluid and silent, like a wolf stalking its prey. His features were obscured by the darkness, but there was no mistaking the cold gleam of his eyes as they locked onto Elara. The hunter had found them.

"Cael," Elara breathed, her voice barely a whisper, the chill of fear running down her spine. "Who is he?"

Cael's hand tightened around the hilt of his dagger, his eyes never leaving the figure before them. "An old enemy," he said, his voice low and steady, though there was a hint of something darker beneath his calm exterior. "One who has been hunting me for a long time."

Elara felt a flicker of dread in her gut as she realized the full extent of what they were facing. This wasn't just a random follower. This was someone who knew Cael, someone who had been tracking them deliberately. And if they had been hunting Cael for so long, there was no telling what they were willing to do to catch him.

The man in the clearing didn't move, his eyes fixed on Cael with an unsettling intensity. There was no smile, no greeting— just the silent, unspoken challenge of two predators locked in a deadly dance.

"You've led her into danger, Cael," the man's voice rang out, cold and measured. His words were a warning, but they were also a declaration. "You know what will happen if you continue down this path."

Cael's jaw clenched, his hand tightening around his weapon. "I didn't come this far to turn back now," he said, his voice low, but fierce. "And neither will she."

The hunter's eyes flickered to Elara for a moment, and in that brief glance, she felt something sharp, like a cold blade brushing against her skin. She could feel the danger radiating from the man, a raw, primal energy that seemed to vibrate in the very air around them.

"You've made a mistake," the man said quietly, almost pityingly. "She doesn't know what she's dealing with. Neither of you do."

Before Elara could react, Cael stepped forward, his movements fluid and precise. The air seemed to crackle with tension, the forest holding its breath as the standoff between the two men stretched on. In that moment, Elara knew—this was more than just a hunt. This was a battle, and whoever won would shape the fate of them all.

And somewhere, deep within her, she knew that her own destiny was tied to this confrontation. She could feel the weight of it—heavy and inevitable. Whatever happened next, it would change everything.

The Heart's Betrayal

The forest had swallowed them whole.

Elara's footsteps echoed in the hollow space between the trees, her breath shallow as she followed Cael deeper into the unknown. The moon, hidden behind a thick veil of clouds, offered no comfort. The only light now came from the faint glow of fireflies, casting fragile, flickering orbs in the distance like cold, unreachable stars. The ground beneath her was soft, moist from the rain, and the leaves seemed to whisper as if sharing secrets with the wind.

Her thoughts were fragmented, torn between the heart-pounding intensity of their escape and the searing confusion of what had just transpired. Cael had moved like a shadow, his every motion fluid, controlled, a stark contrast to her frantic steps. And still, despite the terror that gnawed at her, there was something else—something undeniable—that pulled her toward him. The strange, unsettling attraction that thrummed through her veins whenever they were near, whenever he looked at her with those dark, fathomless eyes, haunted her now more than ever.

But now, as they ventured farther into the forest, she couldn't shake the feeling that something was wrong. The path they had been following was narrowing, the trees growing thicker, their branches twisting overhead in unnatural, almost menacing angles. Her chest tightened, and despite the cool air, the dampness of the night seemed to press in on her, stifling her.

"Cael..." Her voice barely rose above the rustle of the wind. "Where are we going?"

Cael didn't answer immediately. He moved ahead, his steps sure and confident, but his shoulders were tense, his jaw clenched as if every step was carefully calculated, every move a strategy in a game she had yet to understand. When he spoke, it was almost too quiet, as though the forest itself were listening.

"We're almost there," he said, glancing back at her, his eyes briefly meeting hers. There was something in his gaze—something sharp, something unreadable—that made her pulse quicken. "You need to understand what you're getting involved in."

The words hit her like a blow, unexpected and sharp. "What do you mean?" she asked, a flicker of unease creeping into her voice. The silence between them was thick, but his presence filled it, heavy and suffocating.

Cael didn't answer right away. He kept walking, his eyes darting between the shadows of the trees, his movements too precise, too deliberate. She wanted to ask more, to press him further, but she had learned that when Cael was like this—when he grew distant—it was better to keep quiet.

And so she did. But the silence between them only deepened, a gulf she couldn't cross, a growing distance that had nothing to do with space and everything to do with the unseen rift forming between them.

The deeper they went into the forest, the more Elara felt the weight of the night pressing down on her. She couldn't explain it, but there was something… off about the way the trees were closing in, about the way the air seemed to thicken, to grow colder.

And then, just when she thought she might scream from the tension building in her chest, she heard it.

A whisper. A voice carried on the wind, too faint to understand but too clear to ignore.

"Elara…"

Her breath caught in her throat. The voice was soft but unmistakable—her name, spoken as though it were an echo of something long forgotten. Her heart stuttered in her chest, her pulse quickening. The sound was strange, otherworldly, like a memory she couldn't quite place.

She stopped dead in her tracks. "Did you hear that?" Her voice was breathless, a wild edge of panic creeping into her words.

Cael didn't stop. His stride never faltered, but there was something in the way his eyes darkened as he glanced over his shoulder. "Keep moving," he said, his tone urgent but controlled. "It's nothing."

Elara took a hesitant step forward, but the voice lingered in her mind, like a touch, like a call from something just beyond reach. She wanted to turn back, to leave this cursed path and run home to the safety of the village, but her feet felt rooted to the spot, her heart a turbulent storm of confusion and fear.

Another step. Then another. And before she knew it, they had reached the heart of the forest.

The clearing they emerged into was stark, open, a silent void where the trees receded, leaving only a vast, empty space bathed in eerie moonlight. The air here was cold, unnaturally so, and as Elara stepped into it, she felt an immediate sense of foreboding. The trees had parted, but they had also created a barrier—a threshold they had crossed that felt final, irrevocable.

"Here we are," Cael said, his voice low, almost a whisper. His tone was different now, softer, but there was no mistaking the tension in his body, the way his eyes scanned the clearing, as if expecting something—someone—at any moment.

"Elara…" the voice called again, closer this time, clearer, and yet no one was there. The whisper seemed to come from all around her, like a presence just at the edge of her awareness, just beyond her reach.

Her heart thudded in her chest as she looked around, searching for the source, but the clearing remained empty, silent except for the faint rustle of the wind.

"Cael, what is this? Who's calling my name?" Her voice was shaky now, her words tumbling out in a desperate rush.

Cael stepped forward, his hand reaching for hers, his fingers brushing against hers in the briefest of touches. His touch sent a surge of warmth through her, but it was a warmth that felt dangerous, full of uncertainty. She felt the tension between them, the unspoken words, the pull that neither of them seemed able to escape.

"Elara, listen to me," Cael's voice broke through the storm of her thoughts. "This place—it's where the curse was born. The heart of it. The power is tied to you, to your bloodline. And if we don't do this right, if we don't break it now, everything—everything you've known—will unravel."

She looked at him, confusion and fear battling for dominance within her. "What do you mean? What am I supposed to do?"

Before he could answer, the wind picked up, whipping through the clearing like a living thing, carrying with it the scent of something ancient, something forgotten. And then, out of nowhere, a figure appeared before them—emerging from the darkness as if summoned by the very air itself.

It was a woman, tall and elegant, with long dark hair that seemed to shimmer in the moonlight. Her face was pale, her eyes sharp and knowing, and though her features were unfamiliar, Elara felt an instant, chilling recognition—a connection she couldn't explain.

The woman's gaze locked with Elara's, and the air seemed to crackle with tension. The ground beneath Elara's feet trembled, a deep, low hum vibrating through her body, as if the earth itself was alive.

"You've come," the woman said, her voice soft but commanding, as though the words were laden with centuries of meaning.

Elara took a step back, fear clenching her chest, but the woman did not move, did not advance. She simply stood there, her presence overwhelming in its intensity.

"You shouldn't have trusted him," the woman whispered, her voice a slow, deliberate hiss, a whisper meant only for Elara. "Cael's loyalties were never yours to claim. He's playing a game he can't win."

Elara's heart skipped a beat. The woman's words cut through her like a blade. She turned to Cael, but his expression was unreadable, his eyes dark and distant.

"What does she mean?" Elara demanded, her voice trembling,

though she didn't want to admit the fear rising inside her. "Cael?"

But he didn't answer. Instead, he took a step toward the woman, his face hardening as though he had already made a decision.

And then Elara understood.

This was the moment.

The moment where everything—every truth, every lie—came to light.

And she was caught in the middle, unable to escape the twisted web of betrayal that had been woven around her.

Nine

The Final Eclipse

The night was suffocating. The air was thick with the smell of earth and ancient wood, the smell of secrets buried too deep to unearth. The moon hung high above the clearing, its silver light spilling through the gaps in the trees, casting long shadows that stretched out like dark fingers across the forest floor. Elara's pulse raced, each breath she took seeming to grow heavier than the last. The figure before her—the woman who had emerged from the shadows—was no longer just a stranger. She was a force, something primal and ancient, and her words had cut through Elara like a blade.

"You've come," the woman had said, her voice like silk and iron all at once. "But you should never have trusted him."

Elara's stomach twisted, her eyes darting between Cael and the woman. The ground beneath her seemed to vibrate, the air around them charged with an unseen force. The trees around the clearing groaned as if reacting to the tension, and the wind began to whip through the branches, carrying with it a low, haunting hum.

Cael stood frozen, his eyes locked onto the woman with a mixture of defiance and something else—something darker, something more desperate. The soft flicker of moonlight caught his face, casting it in sharp relief, but there was no warmth in his gaze. Only cold calculation.

"What does she mean?" Elara's voice was barely above a whisper, her words trembling with the weight of the question. She turned to Cael, her chest tightening as she tried to read his expression, but there was no answer in his eyes. Just a void.

The woman's lips curved into a smile, and it was the kind of smile that sent a chill straight to Elara's bones. It was a smile of someone who knew something you didn't. Something that was about to destroy everything.

"Cael has kept you in the dark," the woman continued, her voice smooth as velvet. "He has used you, Elara. For what? For power. For control. He thinks he can break the curse—your curse—by using you as a pawn in his game."

Elara's chest tightened painfully, and she stepped back, her heart pounding so loudly in her ears that it drowned out the sounds of the forest. Used her? The words hung in the air like poison, and she didn't know whether to believe them, but the doubt that had started to gnaw at her heart was suddenly like a wildfire, spreading too quickly to contain.

"You're lying." The words escaped her lips before she could stop them. She took another step back, her breath catching in her throat. "He would never—"

But the woman simply smiled again, as though she were savoring Elara's disbelief. "Do you think the curse is just a story? A thing of myth?" Her voice grew colder, sharper. "The truth, Elara, is far darker than you know. The curse you carry is the key to the world, and Cael? He will stop at nothing to claim it."

Elara could feel her head spinning. The world around her seemed to tilt, the air turning thick with tension. She turned her eyes to Cael, searching for any sign, any clue that would tell her that the woman was wrong, that it was all some horrible misunderstanding. But Cael didn't look at her. Instead, he stood motionless, his jaw clenched as though fighting something— something he couldn't let her see.

"You don't understand," he finally spoke, his voice low and tight, as if the words cost him. "You think the curse is just something that can be broken. But the truth is, Elara, you've always been a part of it."

Her heart froze in her chest. "What does that mean?" she asked, her voice shaky, but demanding, like a rope she was trying to pull herself up from the edge of an abyss.

Cael took a step forward, his eyes finally meeting hers. The intensity in his gaze took her breath away, but there was something else there—something that she couldn't quite place, something deep and dark that made her want to recoil.

"You're the vessel," he said, the word heavy, laden with a weight she couldn't comprehend. "You've always been the vessel. The curse wasn't born from just any bloodline—it was born from yours. It's been passed down through generations, waiting for you. The one who would carry it—control it—unlock its power."

The silence between them stretched, a taut, brittle thing. Elara felt the ground shifting beneath her feet, her heart racing as the words sank into her chest like daggers. She wanted to scream, to run, to escape this nightmare that had twisted into something she couldn't fight. But her legs felt like stone. She was rooted in place, as though the forest itself had claimed her.

"Cael… you…" Her voice faltered as the weight of his confession hit her. He had known all along. He had known.

The woman's laugh broke the silence, sharp and cruel. "You see, Elara? He's always known. He's been lying to you, manipulating you. Every step of the way."

"Elara," Cael's voice cut through her thoughts, and she felt her chest tighten, but there was no warmth in it. There was nothing familiar in the way he said her name. "I didn't want this. I didn't want you to get involved. But there's no other way. You are the only one who can wield the power of the curse. You have to understand, I… I did this to protect you."

"Protect me?" she spat, her breath quickening as the adrenaline surged through her veins. "Protect me? You've been using me! You never told me the truth. You never trusted me."

His eyes softened for a moment, a flicker of something akin to regret flashing across his face. But it was fleeting, like a storm that passed too quickly to hold on to. He was torn, Elara could see it now—the man she had come to care for, the man she had trusted, was standing on the edge of something he couldn't control. And she had been drawn into it, helplessly.

"I never wanted to hurt you," he whispered, his voice raw with the weight of the confession. "But you have to know the price. The power you carry, Elara… it comes at a cost."

And that was it. The truth had been laid bare, as jagged and brutal as a broken mirror, each shard cutting into her heart, leaving her bleeding. She had trusted him. She had believed in him. And now, as she stood in the heart of the forest, everything she thought she knew was crumbling.

"You were just a tool to him," the woman hissed, her voice dark and low, like a serpent's whisper. "Nothing more."

But Cael's gaze never wavered from Elara's, and for a moment, she saw the man he truly was—a man trapped by his own choices, a man who had made a deal with darkness long before she ever entered his life. He wasn't the person she had thought him to be.

"I never wanted this for you," he repeated, his voice breaking with something raw. Something human. "I never wanted to drag you into the darkness."

But it was too late for apologies. It was too late for regrets. The truth had been exposed. The curse was not just something he had tried to break; it was something he had always meant to control, to use.

And as the final, brutal piece of the puzzle clicked into place, Elara knew that everything was about to change. That nothing—nothing—would ever be the same again.

Ten

A Crown of Thorns

The moon was a pale, sickly orb high in the sky, its light casting an ethereal glow over the clearing, though it was quickly swallowed by the thickening fog that seemed to rise from the ground itself. The trees surrounding Elara loomed like silent sentinels, their branches gnarled and twisted, reaching out to her like the hands of ghosts, beckoning her into their grasp. The chill in the air had nothing to do with the late hour or the fog. It was the kind of cold that seeped into the marrow, that prickled the skin with a promise of something dangerous waiting just beyond the veil.

Her heart hammered in her chest, and her breath came in short, uneven gasps, her throat tight with fear. She wanted to run. She wanted to flee from the man standing just a few feet away from her—Cael, the man who had once promised her safety, now nothing more than a stranger wearing the mask of someone she used to trust. His betrayal had shattered everything, but somehow, she couldn't walk away.

Her gaze flickered over to him, and for a brief moment, she saw something that looked like guilt flicker in his eyes—quick and fleeting, like a shadow that passed too quickly to catch. But it was gone before she could hold onto it.

He took a step forward, his movements smooth and predatory, his dark eyes never leaving hers. The air between them was thick with tension, like a taut wire waiting to snap.

"Elara," he said softly, his voice hoarse, as if speaking to her cost him more than just words. "I never wanted to hurt you. I never wanted any of this to happen."

She swallowed hard, but the lump in her throat wouldn't go away. "Then why did you?" she asked, her voice barely more than a whisper, but the anger behind the words was unmistakable.

He closed the distance between them in two quick strides, and before she could take a step back, his hand was at her wrist, his fingers wrapping around her delicate skin in a grip that was too tight, too firm. She flinched, but he didn't release her.

"You don't understand," he said, his voice low, the words forced through clenched teeth. "You never could."

Elara's pulse quickened at the touch, not from fear, but from something else—something far more dangerous. Despite the anger and betrayal roiling inside her, there was an undeniable pull toward him, a magnetic force that she couldn't escape. She had felt it from the very first moment they had met, and now, standing on the edge of everything, it was stronger than ever.

"I trusted you," she said, her words biting, a fire in her chest that threatened to consume her. She tried to pull away from him, but he held on, his grip tightening, his thumb brushing against the soft skin of her wrist in an almost intimate touch. The contrast between the hardness of his hand and the tenderness of his touch made her stomach twist.

"Trust is a dangerous thing, Elara," he replied quietly, his voice rough, as though each word cost him. "Especially when it comes to something like this."

Her breath caught in her throat, her eyes searching his face for any sign that he wasn't lying to her, that he hadn't been playing a game from the very beginning. But there was nothing. Only that unreadable look in his eyes, a mix of guilt and something darker. Something real.

"What do you mean?" she asked, her voice trembling, though she fought to keep it steady. "What is this really about, Cael? What have you been hiding from me?"

Cael released her wrist abruptly, stepping back as though he couldn't bear to be so close to her anymore. Elara was left standing there, the cold air biting at her exposed skin, the emptiness of the space between them a physical weight.

"You're right," he said, his voice barely above a whisper. "I've kept so many things from you. But I never meant for you to be part of it. You weren't supposed to be caught in this web." He turned away, his back to her now, his posture rigid, as if he were preparing for something inevitable. "But it's too late now. You're already entangled."

Elara could feel the weight of his words pressing down on her chest, suffocating her. "You can't just tell me this and walk away, Cael," she demanded, her voice stronger now, desperate for answers. "I need to know what you've done. What you've been using me for."

Cael turned slowly, his face grim, his eyes narrowing as if weighing his next words carefully. The seconds stretched into eternity, and for a moment, it felt as though the forest itself was holding its breath.

"I've been protecting you," he said, the words coming out in a rush. "But it was never just about you, Elara. The curse, your bloodline—it's not just a story. It's a power, an ancient force that has been dormant for centuries. And you…" He stopped, his gaze flickering to the ground before meeting her eyes again. "You are the key."

Her heart skipped a beat. "The key?" she echoed, the word tasting foreign on her tongue.

He nodded, his expression tight, as though saying the words out loud made them somehow more real. "The curse isn't just something that haunts your family—it's alive. It's waiting for the right person to unlock its power. And that person is you, Elara."

A wave of nausea swept over her. The weight of his words crashed down on her like a tidal wave. She felt as though the earth beneath her was crumbling, as though the world itself was shifting, and she was powerless to stop it. The key. Her mind couldn't wrap around it. She had thought she was just a victim, a pawn in someone else's game, but now… now she was the game.

"You've been using me," she said, the realization dawning on her like the sun breaking through the dark clouds of a storm. "This whole time… you've been using me."

Cael's face twisted with a mixture of regret and pain, but his voice was steady when he spoke. "I never wanted to hurt you, Elara. But the truth is, there's no one else. You're the only one who can wield this power. And the moment you accept it—" He cut off, his throat tight as if the very thought of it made him choke. "You'll change."

The world around her felt like it was spinning, her thoughts scattered like leaves in a storm. She could feel the weight of the decision pressing down on her, the realization that whatever path she chose now would define everything. The curse. She had always thought it was a myth, something told to scare children into obedience. But now, she realized, it was much worse than that. It wasn't just a curse. It was power. Dangerous, corrupting power.

She met his gaze again, her breath catching in her throat. "You've known all along, haven't you?" she asked, her voice trembling with the force of the question. "You knew what this would do to me. You knew what I would become."

Cael didn't answer right away, and the silence between them grew thick, suffocating. Finally, he spoke, his voice soft, almost a whisper, but full of something raw, something vulnerable. "I never wanted you to be part of this, Elara. But I couldn't stop it. I couldn't stop us."

Her chest tightened as the unspoken words hung in the air, and for the first time, Elara realized just how much of this was tied to her—how much of it was tied to him. The attraction, the pull, the power—they were all part of the same, tangled web. A web she didn't know how to escape.

And in that moment, as the tension between them crackled like lightning waiting to strike, Elara knew that whatever came next, she would have to face it. She would have to decide whether she could trust him again—or whether she had already lost everything.

"I don't know if I can ever forgive you," she whispered, the words bitter in her mouth. "But I can't walk away. Not now. Not when everything is about to change."

Cael's eyes flickered with something like relief, though it was mixed with an unmistakable sorrow. "Then stay with me, Elara," he said, his voice hoarse. "We have to face it together. There's no other way."

And in the stillness of the night, with the world closing in around them, Elara made her choice.

65

Eleven

The Breaking of Chains

The forest was a labyrinth of shadows, each tree twisting like a dark sentinel watching their every move. The mist hung thick around them, a silken veil that distorted everything it touched. The moon was still hidden behind the ever-thickening clouds, leaving the world in a blanket of oppressive darkness. Elara's breath came in quick, shallow gasps as she tried to focus on the path before her, though her thoughts were tangled and chaotic.

They had been walking for what felt like hours, each step taking them further into the unknown. Cael was beside her, his presence a silent weight at her side, his hand occasionally brushing against hers in a fleeting touch that sent a jolt of electricity through her. The attraction, the need to be near him, was undeniable. But with it came something else—something darker that gnawed at her insides, something that whispered of danger at every turn.

Cael hadn't spoken much since they had left the clearing where the woman had revealed the truth. His silence was suffocating, but she could feel the tension in the air between them, an unspoken understanding that something monumental was about to happen. The curse, the power, and the consequences of everything they had set into motion—everything was building to a breaking point.

"Elara," Cael's voice was a low rasp, almost drowned by the sound of the rustling trees and the steady patter of raindrops on the forest floor. "We need to reach the heart of the curse. Time is running out."

His words hung in the air, but they didn't offer her any comfort. Her heart hammered against her ribs as she glanced up at him, her eyes searching his for some sign, something that would reassure her, but all she found was the same determined mask he had worn since she had joined him on this cursed journey.

"I don't understand," she said, her voice trembling slightly despite her efforts to remain composed. "If we're so close, why are we running? Why aren't we doing something?"

Cael's gaze flickered to her, a brief flash of something unreadable passing over his face. For a moment, it seemed like he would say something, but then the moment passed, and he shook his head slightly, the weight of his silence thickening the air between them.

"Because we're not the only ones looking for it," he said finally, his voice low, laced with a tension that made Elara's stomach churn. "There are others who would do anything to claim the power of the curse for themselves. And they won't hesitate to destroy everything in their way to get it."

Her chest tightened, and she stopped walking, her feet sinking slightly into the soft, wet earth as she turned to face him. Her breath came faster now, her hands trembling as she clenched her fists at her sides.

"Cael," she said, her voice rising, filled with a mixture of frustration and desperation. "What is it you're asking me to do? Do you want me to just accept all of this? To embrace whatever this power is that I have inside me? Do you expect me to stand by you while you tear apart everything I know?"

He looked at her then, his gaze dark and conflicted, but there was something else in his eyes—something that made Elara falter, something that made her question everything she thought she knew about him. The hardness in his features softened for a fraction of a second, and in that moment, the distance between them seemed to shrink.

"I never wanted this for you," he said quietly, his voice raw, his eyes holding hers with a painful intensity. "I never wanted to drag you into this… into my fight. But now that you're here, you have to make a choice. The curse—it's in your blood, Elara. And the power inside you… it could either save everything or destroy it."

She opened her mouth to protest, to argue that she didn't want any of it, that she wasn't a weapon to be wielded, but her words died in her throat. There was something in the way Cael spoke, the way he looked at her, that made her feel like she was standing at the edge of a precipice. The truth was, she did have power. She could feel it thrumming beneath her skin, a pulse that had been there from the very beginning, that had been growing stronger with every passing day.

"I can't just ignore it," she whispered, her voice barely audible as she looked down at her trembling hands. "What if I can't control it? What if it destroys everything I love?"

The air between them grew thicker, and for a moment, all they could hear was the sound of the wind rustling through the trees, the distant howl of wolves echoing in the distance.

"Elara," Cael said softly, stepping closer, his voice laced with an intensity that made her breath catch in her throat. "You can control it. You have to. You were born for this. The curse isn't just something that happens to people, it's a force that's been waiting for you to take it, to wield it. You can control it. I know you can."

She looked at him then, her heart in her throat, her chest rising and falling with the effort of holding it all together. There was something in the way he spoke, something so certain, that made her chest ache with a longing she didn't fully understand.

His hand reached for hers, and for a moment, the world seemed to stop. His fingers brushed over hers, the touch light but electric, sending a jolt of warmth through her, as though the very contact ignited something deep within her.

"Cael," she breathed, the word slipping from her lips without thinking.

He was so close now, so close she could feel the heat of his body against hers. She could see the way his jaw tightened, the way his lips parted as though he, too, was struggling with something. She could feel the tension in him, the same pull that had been there from the very beginning. The attraction, the need—it was all-consuming.

"Trust me," he said, his voice rough, the plea in it unmistakable. "I've never asked for anything from you, but I need you now. I need you to trust me, to trust that I'm not leading you into this alone. Together, we can break the chains of the curse. Together, we can end this."

The words hung between them, raw and unspoken, and for the briefest moment, Elara felt the weight of them press down on her chest. Together. It wasn't just the curse anymore. It wasn't just about breaking something ancient and evil. It was about them. About everything they had become since the very first moment they had met in that darkened forest. She was standing at the edge of something she couldn't turn away from.

But was she ready? Could she walk this path with him, knowing what was at stake?

She lifted her chin, her eyes locking with his, and in that

moment, everything else faded away. The trees, the mist, the cold. Everything but Cael. She took a steadying breath and nodded. "I trust you," she said, her voice barely more than a whisper, but the words were heavy with meaning. "I trust you."

And as they stood there, side by side, the wind picking up around them, Elara knew that there was no turning back. No escaping what was to come. The curse was not just a force that threatened them; it was something inside of her now. And she had to face it—had to accept it—for better or worse.

Together.

Twelve

The Moon's Promise

The air was thick with tension, as if the night itself was breathing. The forest stretched before Elara like an endless expanse of shadowed trees, their bare branches reaching toward the dark sky like skeletal hands begging for release. Now fully visible, the moon hung low in the sky, its silver light illuminating the path before her. But the moon's brightness did little to dispel the oppressive sense of dread that weighed heavily on her chest.

She was standing at the edge of a precipice that fate had carved for her, and she didn't know if she was ready to take the final step. Her heart pounded in her chest, so loud in her ears that it almost drowned out the whispers of the wind through the trees. The forest around her felt alive, like something ancient was stirring beneath the earth, something that had been waiting for her to awaken it.

Beside her, Cael moved like a shadow, his presence a constant reminder that there was no going back. His eyes were focused ahead, his expression unreadable, though there was an edge to his movements—an urgency she hadn't seen in him before. The weight of their journey, the magnitude of what they were about to do, seemed to be settling into his bones, and she could see it in the way his jaw tightened, in the way his hands flexed at his sides.

"Elara," he said, his voice low but steady, as if preparing her for something that had already been set in motion. "This is it. This is where it all ends."

Her breath caught in her throat. She turned to him, searching his face for something—some flicker of hope, some sign that what they were about to do wasn't as impossible as it felt. But all she found was the same certainty that had been there since the moment they had set foot in this cursed forest. It was the same certainty that had driven him from the beginning, the same certainty that had both drawn her to him and torn her apart.

"I'm ready," she whispered, though the words felt hollow. She wasn't sure if she was ready. But what choice did she have? They had come this far. She had come this far.

Cael's eyes softened for a moment, and for the briefest of seconds, there was something in them that made her chest tighten—something that made her wonder if he had ever truly wanted to be part of this. But then it was gone, replaced by the cold resolve that she had come to know all too well.

"Are you sure?" he asked, his voice barely more than a breath, but there was something almost pleading in it. "Once you step into this, there's no turning back."

Elara nodded, her throat tight. She knew what he meant. The power within her, the curse that had been passed down through generations of her bloodline, was alive now—alive within her. And if they did this, if they went through with what he was asking, there would be no undoing it. She would either be consumed by the curse or take control of it.

And she wasn't sure she had the strength to control it.

But she wasn't afraid anymore. Not of the curse, not of the power within her. What terrified her now was the unknown. What would she become? And what would Cael think of her after it was all over?

The wind picked up, swirling around them like an invisible force, tugging at the edges of her cloak. It was cold, colder than it had been before, and it made her shiver, though it wasn't the chill of the night that made her body tremble. It was the weight of the decision she was about to make.

The trees around them seemed to whisper, their leaves rustling in the wind, the sound almost like a voice, like something calling to her, beckoning her forward. And in the distance, just beyond the clearing, Elara saw it.

The altar.

It was an ancient stone structure, half-buried in the earth, its surface worn smooth by centuries of weathering. The symbols carved into the stone were old, older than anything Elara had ever seen—symbols that seemed to hum with an energy she could feel deep in her bones. The air around the altar seemed to vibrate, alive with power. She could feel it, pulsing in the ground beneath her feet, calling to her.

"Cael," she said, her voice shaking despite herself. "Is this it?"

Cael nodded, stepping forward, his hand brushing against her arm as he passed. "This is where it all began," he said quietly, his eyes scanning the altar with a look of reverence. "The curse was born here, and it will end here."

The words echoed in the clearing, and Elara couldn't help but feel the weight of them, the finality of it. This wasn't just about breaking a curse. This wasn't just about her family's legacy or her own fate. This was about the very power that had shaped their world—power that had been dormant for centuries, waiting for someone to claim it.

And now, that someone was her.

Cael stopped at the edge of the altar, turning to face her. There was a stillness to him, a quiet calm that made Elara's chest tighten. He was waiting for her, waiting for her to take that final step, to embrace the power that she had been running from for so long.

"Elara," he said, his voice soft, his gaze locked on hers, intense and unwavering. "This is the moment. You can't walk away from this. Not now. Not after everything."

She looked at him, her heart racing in her chest, her eyes searching his face for some sign, some answer to the questions swirling in her mind. Did he really believe in her? Did he believe that she could control this power, that she could make the choice to wield it and not let it destroy her?

But there was nothing in his expression but that same unwavering certainty. He believed in her, and that belief—though it should have comforted her—only filled her with more doubt. What if she wasn't strong enough? What if the power inside her consumed her? What if, after all this, she lost herself in the curse, in the dark forces that had been waiting to claim her for so long?

"Elara," Cael's voice broke through her thoughts, low and insistent. "You have to choose. Now."

Her breath hitched in her throat, and for a moment, she felt like the weight of the entire world was resting on her shoulders. There was no going back now. No more running, no more hiding.

This was it. This was the moment she had been waiting for, the moment she had feared.

She stepped forward, her heart pounding in her chest as she crossed the threshold of the altar. The moment her foot touched the stone, a jolt of power shot through her, a surge of energy that made her whole body tense, as though the very earth beneath her was awakening.

And then, just as she thought she might collapse from the intensity of it, she heard it.

The voice. The voice that had called her before, the voice that had been whispering her name in the wind. It was clearer now, closer. It wasn't just in the wind anymore. It was inside her, echoing through her mind like a forgotten memory.

"Elara," it called again, the sound like a caress, like something ancient and familiar. "You are the one. The chosen. The power is yours to claim."

Her breath caught in her throat, and her knees buckled, but Cael was there, his arms steadying her, holding her as she trembled with the force of it, with the weight of the power awakening inside her. The curse was no longer something outside of her, something to fear. It was part of her now, a part of who she was, and in that moment, she realized that she could not fight it.

She had to embrace it.

"Elara," Cael whispered, his voice just above a breath, as though he, too, was feeling the weight of the moment. "Do you feel it? Do you feel the power?"

She nodded, though the words were stuck in her throat. The power was inside her, overwhelming her, but it wasn't just fear. It was something else—something intoxicating. She could feel it in her veins, in her soul, and for the first time, she wasn't afraid.

She was ready.

"Do it," Cael urged, his hands gentle but firm as they rested on her shoulders, his gaze never leaving hers. "Embrace it."

And in that moment, under the weight of the moon's promise, Elara made her choice.

She raised her arms, and the world around her seemed to shift.